SINGING
FOR
OUR LIVES

SINGING
FOR
OUR LIVES

Positively Gay and Christian

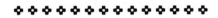

MICHAEL SEAN PATERSON

CAIRNS PUBLICATIONS
SHEFFIELD
in association with
ARTHUR JAMES
BERKHAMSTED
1997

First published in Great Britain by

CAIRNS PUBLICATIONS
47 Firth Park Avenue
Sheffield s5 6HF

in association with

ARTHUR JAMES LTD
70 Cross Oak Road
Berkhamsted
Hertfordshire HP4 3HZ

Further copies of this book and other Cairns Publications
can be obtained from Arthur James Ltd

ISBN 0 85305 420 7

Typeset in Monotype Baskerville
by Strathmore Publishing Services, London N7

Printed by the Ipswich Book Company, Suffolk

For Pablo

whose love has freed
the song of my heart

and for whose life
I now sing

eres tú

The homosexual is endowed with a wealth of religious feelings which help to bring the *ecclesia spiritualis* into reality, and a spiritual receptivity which makes him responsive to revelation.

— *Carl Gustav Jung*

If you want to know what we believe, come and see what we sing.

— *St Augustine*

God is not nice. God is no uncle. God is an earthquake.

— *Hasidic saying*

CONTENTS

Figures in square brackets in the text refer to the Notes starting on page 89.

x

INTRODUCTION

I AM a gay Christian for whom the Roman Catholic community is 'home'. For the past fifteen years I have been engaged in theology and pastoral care. Since 1993 I have been working with CARA, a pastoral and educational ministry to people affected by HIV/AIDS. From 1995 to 1997 I was responsible for pastoral care at London Lighthouse.

The experience of AIDS has changed my life, given me freedom at so many levels and empowered me to sing my own song. In being with positive people (in both senses of the word 'positive'), in sharing our weekly liturgies, in retelling the birth, death, and new-life stories of Christmas and Easter, in accompanying so many to the grave and beyond, and in the many friendships born from our shared plight, I have encountered a spirituality that is both positively gay and Christian and outstrips in authenticity much of my own religious past.

It has been precisely in this community which lives so much on the edge of society and on the fringes (if at all) of established religion that I have discovered anew the warm breath of God and have witnessed a passionate commitment to life lived in abundance. [1] In those whose blood carries both vitality and mortality I have seen a vision of the kingdom as an immanent unfolding reality. I have baptised babies with AIDS, folded forgiveness around lonely friends in confession, [2] shared bread in memory of One whose body was broken, and received the cup of suffering from those for whom the symbol has real presence. I have witnessed and blessed the love that dares to speak its name in rituals of union, and I have buried too many too often with too many emotions and too many unanswered questions. And I have sat, over and over again, with those who speak with undeniable authority of dying and rising and transfiguration.

If I have a ministry to others, it is because my own heart has been broken open through this death-dealing yet life-provoking virus. If I am any nearer to wholeness it is because others have ministered to me.

So I have set about this task of articulating what light AIDS , with all its attendant entourage, throws on life lived in the spirit. I am eager to do this, partly for the experience itself, but also to explore the meaning of all that has happened to me these past few years.

If I have a wider purpose, it stems from realising that the many pastoral and practical responses to HIV/AIDS which have been initiated in the name of Christ have rarely been substantiated in terms of theological and spiritual under-pinnings. The earliest, and sadly ecumenically adopted line, was that of fundamentalists of all persuasions who decreed that AIDS was the wrath of an angry God unleashed on sinners as due punishment for their depraved living. [3] There is no argument here, merely an over-confident claim to know the mind of the Almighty. Such a deceptively simply approach does not merit the term theol-ogy – but that should hardly surprise us, given that funda-mentalism is characterised more by ideology than by theology.

Far from being static and monolithic in its certainty, any adequate Christian theological and spiritual reflection on AIDS must be characterised by a dynamic exploration of the complexity of human reality in the light of God's revela-tion in Christ as experienced through the Holy Spirit, and even then bow before the Utterly Mysterious.

I could not have written this book without the help of a great many people. I particularly want to acknowledge:

all those who have taught me the saving power of story telling – my friends who have gone over the rainbow, and those who live with HIV;

David Randall, who since I first drafted these words has also died, and Gordon Twist who got me into this mess, and CARA and Lighthouse who sustain me in it;

the Society of Jesus who taught me to think for myself and to find God in *all* things;

the Benedictine monks of Elmore Abbey who gave me shelter and silence, and cloaked my writing in prayer;

and Jessica and Richard who nurtured the song within and believed in me –

to you all, a simple but heartfelt: Thank you!

MICHAEL SEAN PATERSON

London, April 1997

FOREWORD

SINGING For Our Lives moves me, provokes me, and tantalises me.

I am moved because I am more than old enough now to have a bit of a sense of history. The generation before mine began the movement for change in civil and ecclesiastical law where it impinges on the lives of gay and lesbian people.

It was largely hidden work, only occasionally public, in the years following the Second World War, and led up to the publication of the Wolfenden Report in the late fifties and the subsequent changes in the law enacted by Parliament in 1967. That quiet movement was totally unbeknown to me as a boy growing up in the 'fifties surrounded by muffled prejudice and an occasional shiver of scandal in the *Daily Express* (my parent's choice, I hasten to add).

I suppose I have to admit to belonging to the next, seemingly now ancient generation, with its heady conferences of the Campaign for Homosexual Equality, the Gay Liberation Front, and, for me, the launching of the then Gay Christian Movement in 1976. Public events, political and celebratory, a recognition of one another ('Not you as well: didn't we keep it all well hidden in those student days of the early sixties?'), the mutual encouragement of solidarity, making a small contribution to the growing literature on gay and lesbian matters, all of these were by definition in the public arena.

Yet the oppressive weight of our earliest years (for me, thirty-three of them), made the personal growing up more difficult and prolonged than the political. It was easier to wear the badges than to be free from all those subtle but consistent messages that to be of homosexual orientation – let alone do anything about it – was to be inherently inferi- or to other human beings. It was hard work to believe in our self-worth, essential for the building of any enduring relationships.

At the same time, because of the courage of the previ- ous generation, we had access to the burgeoning resources of the seventies – organisations, self-help groups, books, film, magazines, clubs. Our lives had more freedom and opportunity because of the contribution of the generation of Antony Grey and his colleagues. It was easy to forget to be grateful to them, understandable that they should feel forgotten – and not a little envious of our opportunities.

Now there is a generation (even two!) younger than me. Heavens, I've swallowed my pride this month and taken out two insurance policies with SAGA, four years after I had qualified by age – and I strive to understand the attractions of shaved heads and nose rings. But I discern a greater self- assurance and maturity at a younger age than was possible for me thirty and more years ago. In my turn I am both pleased and a little envious.

That maturity has a darker and sometimes richer colour to it because of AIDS: darker because of the awfulness, both personally and politically, of the illnesses and the dying, sometimes richer because so many people have demon- strated (and others been impressed and moved by) a fierce love and loyalty that has gradually been convincing families, friends and workmates ˙ that gay and lesbian relationships have a potential for passionate and enduring love that can surprise and challenge heterosexual relation- ships out of their lethargy and predictability.

Michael Seán's book bears witness to the anguish and

achievements of this 'third' generation. If I can say it without sounding too grandfatherly (a word I am beginning to learn how to take to myself!), it is a young man's book (flattery may still get me somewhere), passionate, angry, truthful, loving, searing in its honesty.

Continuing in 'elder' mode, I am not surprised that this book should have provoked me as well as moved me.

A few months ago, Steve Bell produced a cartoon in *The Guardian* that featured his penguins making their usual provocative remarks. A penguin in cassock and surplice was encouraging all the homosexual penguins in the congregation to clap their hands and praise the Lord. Others (presumably in antarctic leather) are invited to shake their chains, Alleluia.

I don't know if Michael Seán supplied Steve Bell with his account of the leather-clad congregation at a funeral, whose chains rattled as heads nodded in agreement with something he had said in his address. But the coincidence says something about the way in which experiences and people that have been kept apart and hidden are now being brought together, however disturbing we find the association.

This particular description (in *Song Fifteen: A Solo Saxophone*) therefore challenges me to think through what can be brought together creatively and not destructively, and what kind of sexual experience and what kind of spiritual experience can be held together in creative tension. A better way of putting it might be to ask what kinds of sexual/spiritual (or 'spirited') experiences enhance human life and enable people to flourish in their loving, and what kinds demean and destroy. Physical rape and sectarian authoritarian leadership are both abuses of power. Yet power is a reality to be negotiated in all relationships.

I suspect that few people have completely recognised and lived through the dynamics of power in those kinds of loving that are particularly intimate and legitimately private. For example, how many of us are clear and secure in making the kind of boundaries for our actions that are both life-protecting and love-enhancing? Further, we have so far become more aware of how men have abused women and children than we have of how women have abused and how men have been abused.

Most gay men know something of the traps of mechanical, anonymous, compulsive sex, with its debasement of true ritual – repetitive patterns of behaviour that have become empty of meaning. We know what it is to be trapped (enslaved?) by the sheer power of sexual desire, especially when an uncomprehending society allows no recognised channels for its expression. So much religious and sexual activity can easily become life-denying and love-avoiding, and I think it is true that those of us who have been deeply committed to the spiritual quest, but within religious institutions, have often found it more difficult to mature in our sexual quest.

And all of us adopt roles, partly to try them out, partly because we experience them as life- and love-enhancing. But they are so only for a time. Then we can easily become trapped by self-imposed limitations. I find myself bothered by uniforms (clerical ones included!) which give people an exaggerated sense of their own importance (perhaps compensating for that deeply ingrained lack of self-worth mentioned earlier) and often place power in their hands which, without the limits of law (public roles) or tenderness (private relationships), easily becomes unbridled. The Gestapo is the obvious example this century, and the Nazi fascist spirit is all too alive and well in Europe (political parties of the Far Right are supported by 25 per cent of the voters of France, Austria, and Italy) for me to be entirely at ease with those who bring the black uniforms and the badges into their sexual relating. Yes, I know the thrill that the exercise of power can give and the excitement that can come from submitting to it, and yes, the boundary of pain and pleasure can be a heady place to inhabit for a while. And I know that love involves the loss of control (but one-sidedly rather than mutually?). Roles and power games can be useful aids to our learning how to grow together, as long as they are contained by trust, affection, and truth, but without the *binding power of love already established in the relationship,* where does excitement stop? Snuff movies?

Similar reflections come to mind as I hear the sound of chain gangs of nineteenth century black slaves in the southern states of America – and even the late twentieth century version of prisoners hewing rocks. We all have a lot of work to do where the issues of power and sexuality are concerned.

That leads me to my third response to this book. My publication blurb refers to these 'songs' as fireworks against the night sky. I have always enjoyed fireworks, ever since I carefully organised my childhood fifth of November by arranging the order in which they were to be lit, saving till last the one I hoped would be the most spectacular. The regular disappointment was that none of them lasted as long as I wished.

So it is with this book. I kept on wanting to say to the author:

'Don't stop there. Take us further, not least into this issue of power. You said at that unusual funeral that if God was not in all of Patrick's life then you didn't know where God was. I want to ask, After due reflection, *how* would you say that God was in all that?

'And what about "survivor" guilt? And the concentration of stigmas around fluids, blood, semen, infection, sex, sexual orientation, disfigurement, the lack of cure, dying, death? And what about those hints of churches gripped by necrophilia, at least half in love with death?

'You have the mind and heart to go deeper. To change the metaphor from fireworks to food, you have given us the hors d'oeuvres. Some of them, many of those involved with the world of gay and lesbian politics, and that of HIV and AIDS, could have anticipated. Others are new, with intriguing tastes. The trouble is that I am now impatient for the main course. I can recognise many of the ingredients that I think you would use. But how are you going to mix them, in what proportion, and with what sauces. And with what flair will they be decorated and served? Don't keep me waiting tantalised for too long – and, with my publishing if not my chef's hat, I should like to be the first to see the recipe.'

JIM COTTER

Sheffield, April 1997

THE WRITING ON THE WALL

IN the summer of 1994 I was asked to address a group of priests and nuns on the topic of the formation of religious sisters and brothers of the future. Given that I was at that time an upwardly mobile member of the Society of Jesus – the Jesuits – the invitation was perhaps not as surprising as it might first seem. I had been trained in theology, I had served as a school chaplain, and I was working on post-graduate studies in spirituality. I went to the meeting with the hard earned confidence of my education and the audacity of my passionately held opinions. But I was in for a surprise. On the wall of the convent which was hosting the gathering was a provocative graffito, 'Your order is meaningless. My chaos is significant.'

Eight stark words, but what a message! I have no idea who wrote it, nor what was meant by it, far less whether the artist was aware of the irony of the statement. But it struck me as more than coincidence that such a message should be preached from the wall of a house sheltering a religious community. Was it the order or the chaos that was outside – and inside?

Like the melody of a song that you cannot get out of your head, that mind-teasing, gut-churning statement took up permanent residence in my consciousness. Whether it was the social comment of an anarchist or the bitter revenge of Attila the runaway Nun, it was literally, for me, the writing on the wall. The more I thought about it and turned it over in my mind, the more it bothered me. What did it mean?

Was it true? Why was it haunting me so? 'Your order is meaningless. My chaos is significant.'

I grew up a liberal but committed believer, passionate about the Gospel and about the Christian community. That commitment lead me to seminary to train as a priest, to spend my energy building grassroots Christian communities in urban Glasgow, to teach Scripture and theology to the native peoples of Guyana, and to co-ordinate the social care of an ecumenical group of churches. And when I realised that I could not save the world through action, I embarked on the way of silence as a Benedictine monk and the way of contemplation as a Jesuit. In my spare time I collected degrees in philosophy, theology, and spirituality.

But by the time I encountered 'the writing on the wall', life had changed radically. What meaning did my *ordered* life have when I was up to my neck in the carnage of so many lives wrecked by the ruthless onslaught on HIV and AIDS? Where was the God of love when all around me so many were dying, rejected by society as outcasts and by the Church as sinners? Where was the community of faith when some of my friends were even being denied Christian burial?

And what role was there for the finer nuances of theological discourse when even the tabloids feigned the zeal of the born again in their crusade to assure the 'innocent' majority that AIDS was God's judgment on 'depraved' behaviour? Is it any wonder that my eyes and heart were drawn to an epigram linking chaos and order, meaning and significance, and that I began to ponder the possibility that all I had held dear in terms of faith, religion, theology, and ministry might in truth be irrelevant, that significance was to be found elsewhere?

Among the twenty dictionary definitions of the word 'order' we find these: 'the condition in which everything is in its right place','tidiness', and 'a state of peaceful harmony'. The entry for 'chaos' is more succinct: 'the formless matter supposed to have existed before the creation of the universe' and 'utter confusion'. Sixteen years into this AIDS pandemic, I am left in no doubt as to which of these two words is the more familiar, has meaning, bears significance.

According to the book of Genesis, to be in chaos is the re-live the beginning of things, to be there on tiptoe seconds before God speaks the creating word. It is to feel the heat of the Spirit as She broods and swirls and hovers over the unknown. It is to be present in awe and wonder when the unimaginable beauty of the new creation emerges out of the void. And to think that we resist it!

I wonder if our preference for 'order' and our dis-ease with 'chaos' point to something of profound importance for our spirituality today, namely our desperate desire to control and to be in control. If we can arrange everything, whether arranging time off work to move house, or deciding where to spend our summer holidays, we know where we are and we feel we have a firm handle on events. But along comes the unexpected, the deal falls through, the tour company goes bust, and everything is in chaos again. More important, what happens when that loss of control is about the bankruptcy of those categories which once served us so well, those ways of understanding the world and our place within it, when the 'faith of our fathers' will no longer suffice, when old answers have no bearing on the new questions?

The prevailing chaos of HIV/AIDS looks set to be around for a good while yet. We can fight it or we can embrace it. If we fight it, it is sure to beat us. Dare we allow it to convert us from the frenzied illusion of being *in control* to the pregnant waiting of a people *on tiptoe*? After all, that is what most of the world has to do, and does not Christianity claim to have thrown in its lot with the powerless. On tiptoe, let us go back to basics.

Part One

Only connect
the passion and the prose
and both will be exalted
and human love will be seen at its height.
Live in fragments no longer.

– E. M. Forster, *Howards End* [4]

LIKE IT WAS

Charley, why can't it be like it was?
I liked it the way that it was ...
I don't know who we are any more.

Look at us, Charley,
Nothing's the way that it was.
I want it the way that it was!
Don't you remember? It was good.
It was really good. [5]

THOSE of us who were brought up as Christians have been treated to more than our fair share of sermons and catechism classes on sin in general and original sin in particular. Those to whom we were entrusted for our education seemed to have an obsession with the 'good old days' before it all went wrong; they tended to blame everything that has happened since on the Fall: the fall of creation and the fallen status of human nature. But much more *original* than sin is original goodness: the goodness of creation, the goodness of human nature, the blessing of it all, the beauty of our beginnings. [6]

According to the book of Genesis, God makes Adam by touching, by handling, by fondling and then awakens him to life through a kiss. The God to whom nothing is impossible chooses to kiss Adam into existence. God's kiss must have been a real smacker, one of those long passionate juicy kisses that would bring anyone to life, to have effected the transition from a lifeless mass of bones and sinews into the vibrant and fleshy Adam. (Actually, the text says that God 'breathed into his nostrils the breath of life': you have to be close to be able to do that!)

But Adam is lonely. He feels himself in harmony with all of creation and has no fear or sense of danger living so closely with wild beasts. He seems to get on well with the animals, and gives each one of them a name. But still, something is missing. He feels lost and lacks a companion. In steps the divine *Jim'll Fix It*, leaving Adam well chuffed. Wow! 'This indeed is bone from my bone and flesh from my flesh.' The rest of creation has got nothing on this. We could not belong together more than we do. As the refrain in the first chapter of Genesis has it, 'God saw that it was good.'

And you can imagine Adam and Eve exploring each other just like little boys and girls do in the bath, asking each other, 'What is that for?' and 'Why haven't you got one?' … and touching … and stroking … and playing … and having no shame or embarrassment or inhibition. Genesis goes on to say that God and Adam walk together in the cool of the evening. You can imagine God asking Adam what he thinks of his new friend, or Adam asking God, 'Where did you find her?'

Then something awful happens, something so terrible that it shatters all the unity, all the harmony that has characterised the story so far. They eat of the forbidden fruit and immediately tension and disharmony enter the scene. In that instant the worlds of nature and of humanity fall out with each other and Adam abandons the poetry of his original song, 'bone of my bone and flesh of my flesh' for the banal accusation, 'It's all her fault – she gave the apple to me.'

8

As if that is not bad enough, the friendship with God also breaks down. The next time Adam and Eve hear God in the garden, they hide because they are afraid. And God calls out to them with a question: 'Where are you?' Adam replies, 'I heard you in the garden, but I was afraid because I was naked. So I hid.' And God says, 'Who told you you were naked?'

This is the first of many times in the Scriptures that we find God questioning humanity, none more than these worth pondering and taking to ourselves. Can you hear the depth of God's sadness in those questions, 'Where are you?' 'Who told you that you were naked?'

You might want to say that Genesis is only a story and is not worth much historically. But is it not true that sometimes the simplest of stories convey the deepest of truths? Isn't it true that we too were made by touching, by the erotic movement of two bodies, by the warm touch of flesh, at best in a moment of mutual passion and love between our parents, at least in a moment of sexual hunger or sheer duty. And isn't it true that we too were kissed into life, were made for Paradise, for harmony with God, with nature, with each other? But what happened? Who told us we were naked? How true it is that so many of us no longer feel comfortable in our 'birthday suits' and hide behind the camouflage of fig leaves. But who told us to hide? The fig leaf industry has expanded enormously since Genesis but still enjoys the custom of those who would conceal their shame, guilt, awkwardness and dis-ease behind the fig leaves of denial, career, alcohol, drugs, education or public image.

Henri Nouwen encapsulates this well. 'The tragedy is that we are so possessed by fear that we cannot see our innermost selves as an intimate place to come home to. We try to find that intimate place in knowledge, competence, notoriety, success, friends, sensations, pleasures, dreams or artificially induced states of consciousness. Thus we become strangers to ourselves, people who have an address but who are never home and hence can never be addressed by the true voice of love.' [7]

What are *your* fig leaves? What do *you* feel you have to hide?

What if we dared to accept that our immediate home is within our own bodies, right here in our own skin? What if we dared to embrace the truth that we are not *no*-body but *some*-body, and that rather than wasting so much energy trying to suppress our physical needs, urges and desires, we actually, at least sometimes, celebrated our *body*-liness?

At the very heart of Christianity is the astonishing claim that God became *fully human* in Jesus and took on human flesh – with a body, erections, ejaculations, sexual attractions, with eyes that noticed beauty, with skin sensitive to the massage of oil and the touch of a woman's hair, with spittle that he rubbed on the eyes of a man born blind, with a taste for a good wine, and with feet that could dance the night away at a wedding feast in Cana.

If we take the Incarnation seriously, if we really believe that God has said Yes to our physicality, our sexuality, in the embodiment of the person of Jesus, then we can dare to peel off the fig leaves that we have become so accustomed to wearing. We can celebrate

the fire, flesh, and blood of our bodies,
longing and the desire,
reaching out and the yearning,

great hunger and loneliness and getting hurt,
gentleness and tenderness,
ecstasy and passivity in the waiting to receive
   love in the empty places desiring to be filled,
an ebbing and a flowing,
a holding in and a letting go again,
mysterious pull of tides and waves of stillness
and turbulence,
surging, sweeping energy,
intense delight
fierce gentleness of communion and of affirmation,
acceptance and sustenance of our tragedy
and vulnerability.

The question then presses, Is this *sexuality* or is it *spirituality*? Is this *bodiliness* or *holiness*? And is there a difference? Is this not what Jesus took to himself in the Incarnation? In Jesus, God shows us holiness in the flesh. In him, bodiliness is already holiness and holiness must always be bodily. Grace is carnal and carnality is graced. Holiness comes through the flesh. Therefore if God is *not* in all of this, then I don't know where God is, since it follows from the Incarnation that fear and denial of sexual embodiment is fear and denial of God.

Adam and Eve hid from God because they were naked, afraid and ashamed of their own sexual embodiment. Sadly the legacy of fear and shame they bequeathed us is alive and kicking in many religious people today. I know. I bear the bruises! At times, religion itself seems not only to be hiding from God but also to be hell-bent on using the Creator as the biggest fig leaf of all behind which centuries of guilt and self-loathing might be concealed.

PART ONE: ONLY CONNECT

What happened to the way it was, Charley?
I liked it the way it was!
Don't you remember?
It was good. It was really good.

Song Two

REWRITING EVERY LINE?

Could it be that it was all so simple then?
Or has time rewritten every line?
If we had the chance to do it all again,
Tell me, would we, could we? [8]

WAS it all so simple then? *Has* time rewritten every line? Is the memory of twenty centuries of sexual embodiment and Christian spirituality too painful to remember? Adrienne Rich speaks in one of her poems of 'the damage that was done and the treasures that prevail'. That epitomises the Church's attempt to struggle with the inherent goodness of sexuality. A lot of damage has been done but a lot of treasures do prevail.

John McNeill, a former Jesuit hounded out of the Order for his reconciliation of gay sexuality and Christian spirituality, offers this litmus test against which to judge our Christian inheritance. Speaking as a professional psychotherapist he notes:

> From a therapeutic point of view the primary issue concerning religious belief systems is not whether they are true or false but whether they provide a support system that allows healthy development in the individual and in the family, or do the belief systems themselves operate in such a way that they are a source of pathology? [9]

Let us unfold the Christian sexual belief system, admitting the damage that was done, recognising the inherent pathologies, while not losing sight of the treasures.

On the whole the Bible has a healthy attitude to sexuality, and shows no prudishness or hesitancy in discussing it. The Song of Songs is an incredibly graphic description of two people who are passionately in love with each other. For centuries commentators interpreted it as the love of God for his people, but nowadays the majority view is that it is demonstrating sheer delight in the erotic.

Ezekiel 23 is even more explicit and goes into graphic detail over a woman's nipples and the fondling of breasts. Verse 20 describes the Egyptian men as 'hung like donkeys, ejaculating as violently as stallions.' Even though the context is the inordinate sexual behaviour of Israel's enemies, it is still surprising to find such explicit descriptions, especially when you realise that the biblical texts went through a considerable editing process. [10]

Much as I would love to, I cannot get away without at least mentioning that gnarled chestnut, Sodom and Gomorrah. Despite everything you have ever heard from priests who seemed to get all hot and sweaty under the collar on the subject, modern biblical scholarship interprets Genesis 19 as actually about the inhospitality of a people towards strangers, and nothing whatsoever to do with gay love. If there *is* any sexual reference, it is to gang rape and to Lot's willingness to let his daughters be abused.

To those who seem to have spent a long time learning by heart the Leviticus passage condemning men lying with men, I would point out the laws governing menstruation, the eating of pork and shellfish and blemishes of the skin. If you are going to adhere to the law, integrity demands that you do not pick and choose. Many kinds of behaviour that were thought disordered then are no longer thought to be so now. It is much clearer to acknowledge that when the

Scriptures are read in their historical context, we find that our understanding of homosexuality as a permanent way of being and of loving is simply not known.

The Old Testament texts which condemn homosexual sex were all written when the people of Israel were continually threatened by larger and more powerful neighbouring tribes. In such a situation all sexual activity had to be procreative. The seed was quite simply needed to make more Jewish babies to swell the remnant that would then be better able to withstand further attack. [11]

In the New Testament, Paul, who is never short of a strong opinion on any subject whatsoever, is remarkably candid when he admits: 'Concerning celibacy, I have no instructions from the Lord. I merely give you my own opinion.' And that turns out to be 'better to marry than to burn' – i.e. if you can't control your sexual passions then marry rather than find yourself in hell! But while few contemporary Christians would heed his advice about the length of a man's hair or a woman's subjection to her husband, voices clamour together to recite his homophobic barrage. Isn't it strange how what he says about haircuts and the place of women is not so divinely inspired – and therefore applicable – as his hostility to queers?

With the early Fathers of the Church, ambiguity enters the scene. On the one hand the place of the body in the pursuit of holiness receives a powerful underscoring in ascetic practices. Here we have a clear statement of the interconnectedness of the body and of the spirit, in that certain bodily acts, such as fasting, self-discipline, going without sleep, were thought to have bearing on spiritual growth. But this attitude is ambiguous in that, while the body spirit interconnection is beyond dispute, the basic

15

attitude towards the body is at best one of suspicion. [12] Various theories have ben espoused as to why this should be so, including the influence of Gnosticism, which held that things in the material realm were evil, while those of the spiritual remained good. It therefore followed that since sex pertained to the material, physical world, it was evil, and that procreative sex led to the trapping of a soul in an evil body.

Legislation against homosexual practices first raises its ugly head at the Council of Elvira in 300 CE, and is strengthened with the imposition of the death penalty for anal sex in 342, specified as death by burning in 390. With Theodosius, homosexuality came to be seen as contrary to the demands of faith and he therefore levied a charge of heresy and treason. [13]

In the sixth century, Justinian intensified the scape-goating. According to him, gay men were responsible for famines, earthquakes and plagues. Therefore they were subjected to torture, mutilation and castration.

Our gay ancestors in the Dark Ages underwent excommunication, denial of last rites, castration, torture, mutilation, being burnt alive and burial in unsanctified ground. The Middle Ages used the word 'sodomy' as a synonym for heresy, so inextricably linked were these two concepts in the popular mind. Thomas Aquinas, writing in the thirteenth century, set the tone for ensuing centuries by insisting that all sexual activity must tend towards procreation. Masturbation or homosexual acts which clearly did not serve that end were 'sins against nature'. Taking his point to the extreme, Aquinas went so far as to place rape on a higher and more acceptable plane than masturbation, arguing that at least the spilling of the seed in rape might result in procreation, to which masturbation could never aspire.

And so it goes on. This is the *support system* that we gay Christians have inherited. This is the air we have breathed for centuries and in which we attempt to grow and mature as healthy, loving, faith-filled adults. This is how our sexuality and our spirituality have met. John McNeill had a point about belief systems that operate in such a way as to be a source of pathology. So did Barbra Streisand when she sang: 'What's too painful to remember we simply choose to forget.' We gay Christians need to heed them both.

SLIP, SLIDING AWAY ...

Slip sliding away, slip sliding away.
you know the nearer the destination
the more you slip sliding away. [14]

FEW words are currently banded around so loosely and
indiscriminately as the term 'spirituality'. Within the
Christian Church we hear of 'liberation spirituality', 'feminist spirituality', 'creation spirituality'. Within society at
large there is evidence of a growing interest in 'New Age'
spirituality, spirituality for the 'new man', and the all pervasive *Twelve Step* spirituality. There has even been talk of the
'spirituality of Guardian readers'! Spirituality, whether theologically or commercially defined, is a growing industry
with its own emergent language, economy and adherents.
But what is it?

Writing in *A Dictionary of Christian Spirituality*, Gordon
Wakefield defines 'spirituality' as 'a word which has come
into vogue to describe those attitudes, beliefs, and practices,
which animate people's lives and help them to reach out
towards supersensible realities. In that same work, S. H.
Evans notes that 'spirituality is used to indicate the recognition that the way we are with ourselves and the way we are
with other people, depends upon the way we are with
God.' [15]

An alternative, perhaps more existentialist understanding, is offered by John Fortunato in *AIDS: The Spiritual
Dilemma:*

> By spirituality I allude to the journey of the soul – not to religion itself but to the drive in humankind that gives rise to religion in the first place. I have in mind the software on the computer of life, not its hardware, the programs it runs, not the data to be input or the machine that processes it or even the printout. By *spirituality* I am referring to that aura around all of our lives that gives what we do meaning, the human striving toward meaning, the search for a sense of belonging.
> [16]

These two citations read together succinctly illustrate two divergent views around spirituality. The former explicitly identifies within the ambit of spirituality 'supersensible realities', the numinous, the other, God. The latter, while employing the traditional language of the soul, is silent on issues of self-transcendence and focuses rather on matters of meaning and belonging.

Herein lies the tension. Is it not true that one could devote one's entire life to the search for meaning and for a felt sense of belonging without ever acknowledging, let alone experiencing 'spirit'. Surely the contemporary canonisation of psychotherapy, and the self-help circuit of workshops and literature, bear eloquent witness to this? But does such merit the appellation *spirituality*?

If there is any currency left in the term, if it is to escape what A. G. N. Flew called 'death by a thousand qualifications', then no matter how much it slips and slides, 'spirituality' must remain connected to its own etymological umbilical cord. If it is about anything, it is about a human person's participation in and response to the very 'pneuma' (spirit-breath) and 'dunamis' (life-energy) of God, that breathing, pulsating, dynamic Life-Force at the heart of the universe. We know God's breathing within us in our longing for communion with each other and with Ultimate Reality. Our own inner yearnings, stirrings, ebbings and flowings, our capacity for great tenderness and harmony, our search for rest, all bear the hallmarks of the spirit within. Whether we call this reality God, Higher Power, Cosmic Spirit or by some other name, let us neither downplay nor compromise the 'spirit' in our 'spirituality'. Without it that spirituality is void and dissolves into another term for 'world-view', 'adopted stance' or 'philosophy of life'.

In saying this I am not suggesting that spirituality is one dimensional, still less that it can be exactly replicated regardless of age, society, culture or personal circumstances. Quite the contrary. As Segundo Galilea writes:

> 'There can be a plurality of spiritualities due to the fact that any authentic Christian spirituality has a human face. The uniqueness of gospel spirituality is fashioned in new ways, and expressed in new forms where different social and cultural contexts, different human and Christian experiences, different faiths and pastoral challenges introduce fresh accents, underline fresh themes and create fresh sensitivities and expressions. Strictly speaking, no Christian spirituality is a 'spirituality of something'; it is always 'of the gospel.' But the gospel experience is lived in different cultures and situations.' [17]

That spirituality is inculturated and situational is nothing new. In the context of fourth century Constantinian Christendom, desert asceticism emerged as a lay protest movement concerned with living the radicality of the gospel without capitulating to the whims of the Emperor. In our own day, in the context of male dominance and patriarchal systems, feminist spirituality has arisen in an attempt to recreate an approach to God which is true to women's experience of embodiment, human inter-connection, and grace.

Liberation theologies which emerged from Latin America in the 1960s and 1970s strongly emphasised that theology and spirituality must be in dialogue with and respond to the particular set of human circumstances in which the community of faith finds itself. The fresh accents, themes, sensitivities and expressions of Christian spirituality reflect the community situation as it struggles towards gospel-living and gives the perennial kingdom message an historical human face. What I am suggesting here is that within the community of gay men affected by HIV and AIDS, Christian spirituality is once more being re-imaged, recreated, renewed. In a very particular and criti-cal historical context, life in the spirit is being given a new face, flesh and blood in a manner that has significance not only for those most directly affected but for the whole People of God. It is to gay men's experience that we now turn.

Song Four

IN AN ALIEN LAND

By the rivers of Babylon, we hung up our
    harps.
For there our gaolers asked us for songs,
our oppressors for joy. Saying:

'Sing us one of the songs of Zion.'
But how could we sing the Lord's song
In an alien land? [19]

– from Psalm 137

STORY-TELLING has a central place in the Judaeo-Christian world. Through the process of active remembering we constitute ourselves as a people with a common heritage and identity. As the Passover Seder recalls, it was not merely our ancestors but *we ourselves* who were slaves in Egypt, *we* who crossed the Red Sea victorious, *we* who were delivered by the outstretched arm.

As members of the Christian community, when we gather in remembrance of Jesus to break bread and to renew our commitment to wash each other's feet, his presence is no mere memory but an immediate reality. As Luis Dupré puts it, 'memory recollects history into auto-biography.' [18] In other words in the gathering together of our fragmented selves and past experiences we find our identity, discover who we truly are and know the inter-weaving of our lives in community.

The sharing of stories, the 're-membering' of

fragments, and the coming together in community have each contributed to the emancipation of gay people from the lonely, shame-filled world of their unspoken secret. The gay novelist Paul Monette who died in February 1995 of an AIDS-related illness, encapsulates our experience so well.

> Everyone else had a childhood where they were coaxed and coached and taught all the shorthand. Or that's how it always seemed to me, eavesdropping my way through twenty-five years, filling in the stories of straight men's lives. First they had their shining boyhood, which made them strong and psyched them up for the leap across the chasm to adolescence, where the real rites of manhood began.... And every year they leaped further ahead, leaving me in the dust with all my doors closed, and each with a new and better deadbolt. Until I was twenty-five, I was the only man I knew who had no story at all. I'd long since accepted the fact that nothing ever happened to me and nothing ever would. That's how the closet felt, once you've made your nest in it and learned to call it home. Self-pity becomes your oxygen. [19]

Monette eloquently describes the 'internal exile', 'disease', 'home-less-ness', 'ventriloquism' and 'learning to pass as straight' which lead to the bleak, constricted, narrow 'coffin world of the closet' so familiar to gay men.

To grow up gay was for many of us to grow up with an all-pervading sense of otherness. To grow up Christian and gay meant that we experienced that otherness as an obstacle to communion not only with the world at large but also with the Wholly Other. Exile, wilderness, apartness seemed to be our lot. There was no ark to save us from the flood since only heterosexual couples were invited on board to ensure the continuation of the species. And that ruled us out! Some of us took refuge in the allegation (or was it fantasy?) that David really did love Jonathan and that John was indeed the beloved disciple. At such moments we held on to the possibility that there might well be room for our sort in the kingdom after all. But largely we were not convinced. Our churches bequeathed us the conviction that we were sinful. Society told us we were criminal and sick. Then AIDS came along, and fingers were pointed, voices were raised, and some of us retreated further into those only half-abandoned closets from which we were so tentatively emerging.

How, where, when could we sing the Lord's song? Who would come close enough to teach us the tune? With whom could we dare to compose a new melody that fitted our experience? And if we did, would anyone sing with us? Were we doomed to be forever alone? Most of us made a brave attempt to sing others' songs, to live their lives, love their loves. Some tried so hard that they died inside. Some were killed for refusing to try. Others gave up trying and took their own lives. And between us we tried every variation on every theme imaginable, but inevitably the key, pitch, rhythm and tempo were irreconcilably out of sync, the harmony discordant, the blending of our voices with those of a hostile society and an intransigent Christian tradition, cacophonous.

And why? Because of the stigma, prejudice, and rejection – partly imagined, partly real – of a society and Church that simply could not and would not cope with our being different, with our audacious cry 'I am what I am.' At root both Church and society seem to live under the dark shadow of fear, particularly sexual fear which compels us to 'reject that which we cannot manage (and) condemn what we do not understand. We set up a means of control to render powerless those dynamic realities we know to be powerful. No aspect of our humanity is invested with more

24

anxieties,yearnings, emotions and needs than is our sexual nature. So sex is a major arena in which the prejudice of human beings finds expression.' [20]

And if this is so of sexuality in general, how much more true it is of those whose sexualities differ from the norm? Is it any wonder that gay men are accustomed to closets, and bushes and drag? Hiding is the easier and more familiar option.

> You gotta to be taught to hate.
> You gotta be carefully taught.
> — *South Pacific*

Psychotherapy is quick to point out that people only have the defence mechanisms that they need. It also tries (in vain) to reassure those on the receiving end of others' aggression that phobias are not in fact amenable to rational argument. Homophobia, which is currently enjoying a new and highly suspicious lease of life, is no exception. In the fear, rejection and scapegoating of homosexuals we see a rare confluence of the murkiest waters of Church and society. With regard to the latter, Hitler's attempted annihilation of 'the men with the pink triangle' (hardly ever mentioned alongside those, even more horrifically treated, with the yellow star) speaks for itself. Sadly the churches' track record is little better. It is a matter of historical fact that religious systems, Christianity, Judaism and Islam included, have been the major institutional legitimisers of compulsory heterosexuality and the punishers of those who did not, would not, or could not conform to that sexual norm. Christianity has continuously sanctioned homophobia. Methods have indeed changed but beneath the pastoral veneer of tolerance, punishment is still the reality.

Homophobia has at its roots something much more widespread, namely 'erotophobia', the deep fear of sexuality and especially of sexual pleasure. The churches seem just about able to cope with genital sexuality as long as it is at least potentially directed towards *baby-making*, whereas gays and lesbians point to the sufficiency in itself of *love-making*. It is only comparatively recently that the churches have managed to speak of a 'unitive' as well as a 'procreative' dimension of sexual love-making for married couples. Gay theology would ask the Church to consider a third dimension, the 're-creative', which sees sex as participating in God's playful delight in creation and therefore as *very, very good*. It would appear that whether consciously or otherwise, the churches' stance is underpinned by an unchallenged tendency to associate creativity and life with heterosexuality, and whatever is unnatural, sick and deadly with homosexuality.

HIV and AIDS, while by no means confined to homosexuals, are popularly so associated in the public mind. So when society confronts a person with HIV/AIDS it comes face to face not only with an understandable abhorrence of the illness but also with its own prevailing ambivalent sexual attitudes. Thus gay people living with HIV/AIDS suffer from a double dose of stigmatism, for they not only challenge the contemporary tyranny of the perfect body, and are seen as a health risk to society, but also threaten the heterosexist imperialism and family-centred myopia of the churches. [21]

One of the graces of working in AIDS ministry is witnessing the empowerment of those gay men and women who have refused to tidy up the mess their presence and sexuality create in the Christian community. Rather than walking out on the Church, some have been able to turn the other cheek and boldly affirm that their story is also a story of salvation, their song a canticle of liberation, their living and loving a manifestation of the transforming and creative power of the life-giving Spirit. Such would agree with Monette:

> Our stories have died with us long enough. We mean to leave behind some map, some key, for the gay and lesbian people who follow – that they may not drown in the lies, in the hate that pools and foams like pus on the carcass of our land. [22]

That many choose to stay and tell those stories within the churches never ceases to amaze me. That one gay man with an AIDS diagnosis has actually asked me to prepare him for reception into the Roman Catholic Church, leaves me speechless!

TELL ME IT'S NOT TRUE

Tell me it's not true. Say it's just a story,
From an old movie of so long ago,
from an old movie of Marilyn Monroe. [23]

– from *Blood Brothers*

TELL me it's not true ...

... that around 22 million men, women and children have been infected by the Human Immune Deficiency virus (HIV).

... that 6.5 million live with Acquired Immune Deficiency Syndrome (AIDS). [24]

... that in Britain alone, over 10,000 have died as a result of AIDS-related illness.

... that more than 9 million children have been orphaned because of AIDS. [25]

... that while the infection rate is rising among hetero-sexuals, the majority of people living and dying with AIDS in the western world are gay men.

Tell me it's not true ...

... that HIV is here to stay.

... that there is no cure.

... that the UK government's 7 per cent cut in funding will not make a difference.

... that society is suffering from compassion fatigue.

Tell me it's not true...

... that AIDS affects partners and carers, mums and dads, brothers and sisters, grannies and grandads, nieces and nephews.

... that it stirs up a hornet's nest of sexuality and identity.

... that disability, disfigurement and diminishment often come with it.

... that even death itself is previewed in the multiple losses of employment, accommodation, income and support structures.

Tell me it's not true ...

... that AIDS provokes feelings of fear, ignorance, disgust, hostility, rejection, marginalisation and prejudice.

... that AIDS comes as 'a visitor of death'. [26]

... that AIDS strikes at the vulnerable – the African

peoples, gay men, intravenous drug users, commercial sex workers, haemophiliacs.

... that those who live with AIDS personally *embody* the rejection of a society hungry for a scapegoat.

... that people with AIDS carry the can for all that society cannot face up to.

'Tell me it's not true ...
    Say it's just a story ...'

Song Six

THOSE WERE THE DAYS

> Once upon a time there was a tavern where
>   we used to raise a glass or two,
> where we used to pass away the hours and
>   think of all the good things we would do.
> Those were the days my friend, we thought
>   they'd never end.
> We'd sing and dance for ever and a day.
> We'd live the life we chose. We'd fight and
>   never lose.
> Those were the days, oh yes! those were the
>   days. [27]
>   – Gene Raskin

THE year – 1969. The tavern – Stonewall. The city – New York. The fight – homophobia. The prize – gay emancipation. Those were the days, oh yes, those were the days, and sure, we thought they'd never end. Back then, many of us began to emerge Lazarus-style, from the stench-filled tombs we called 'home' in which we had perfected the art of the living dead. I am sure I was not the only one who had not quite completed the marathon task of peeling off the bandages which clung so tightly when friends started to get sick and all hell was let loose. Panic gripped society and the gay community. Rumours spread like wildfire. It was HTL III, GRID, a gay plague or, as those with a graphic bent put it, 'Arse Injected Death Sentence'.

Whatever it was *then*, whatever we call it *now,* in some ways the carnival *is* over. How could we sustain our boisterous confidence when all around us members of our tribe were dropping like flies as AIDS took its ruthless toll? Sure, we still meet in taverns, and still raise a glass or two, but now it is to drown our sorrows. Our jubilation is tempered by the empty bar stools to left and to right and by the collection tins which have become part of the furniture. Remember! Resolve! Respond! – the three R's symbolised in the Red Ribbon – how could we forget? AIDS is now so much part and parcel of our identity as gay men that few among us can remember what life was like before it came to stay. Those were the days, oh yes, those were the days!

For anyone in the prime of life, the dawning consciousness of living under the shadow of a life-threatening illness is likely to provoke an acute crisis. The order on which we had depended has proved unreliable; we are too stunned by the ensuing chaos to ascertain its significance. We need time to mourn our losses. Returning from his first HIV-related hospitalisation, David wrote this song for his partner Adam as he lay sound asleep beside him.

> Sadly, all there should have been
> and all the love we could have seen
> and all our hopes
> and all our dreams
> will soon be swept away.
> I wanted to grow old and grey
> with you beside me every day.
> I love you more than words can say
> but sadly fate is taking this away. [28]

I doubt if David knew just how quickly all *would* be swept away and that his final tribute to Adam would be premiered at his own funeral a few months later.

It is not only sad; it also hurts. How often have I sat with lonely friends in genito-urinary clinics as they await the news that could change their lives. Thankfully the situation has improved from the early days when we held our breath for the two-week interval between HIV test and result. Nor need we fear a result in the post or worse still casually over the telephone as our elders experienced. But it still hurts. It hurts to see the faces of those who have been given the all-clear trying to conceal their relief as they glide through the waiting-rooms, guilt-ridden that they will survive. In this time of AIDS many of us are no longer sure whether it's better to be HIV-positive or negative. The scientific fact which divides us on either side of that continuum seems arbitrary and pedantic given that this virus has shattered the hopes and dreams of *all* gay men. You do not have to have tested antibody-positive to be overtaken by anger, remorse or bouts of real despair. Wendy, whose daughter lives with HIV, speaks for many:

> The weight of this fathomless black bears down upon me.
> I need words as my searchlight,
> my direction out of this inarticulate nothingness
> where I am preyed upon by my own silence.
>
> I strain against the darkness.
> I sense no hands, no faces, no other.
> The air is thick with used worn phrases that
> long, long ago lost their meaning ...
>
> I am left alive on the inside of this explosion.
> I open my throat to explain ...
> ... but remain mute. [29]

Human crises are not always pathological disasters. They can also be opportunities for change, action and

33

growth. Crises stimulate us to ask new questions about the meaning of our lives and to seek new intellectual and behavioural responses. Kierkegaard described crises as leading to

> the moment when a person suddenly grasps the meaning of some important event in the past or future in the present; this grasping of the new meaning always presents the possibility and necessity of some personal decision, some shift in gestalt, some new orientation of the person toward the world and the future.' [30]

Testing HIV-positive can be such a moment of 'kairos' in a person's life, an invitation to restructure his whole life, to ask the fundamental existential questions that most of us put off for another day and to discover and articulate his deepest desires for life. If this is not the stuff of spirituality, what is? Many people experience their diagnosis as a crossroads, one path of which is characterised by the helpless, hopeless, victim-culture of those *dying* of AIDS. The other finds its manifesto in Maya Angelou's words: 'The question is not how to survive, but how to thrive, with passion, compassion, humour and style.' [31]

As one HIV-positive man told me:

> This virus has given me my life. I used to cruise along at lightning speed without a care for myself, never mind anybody else. If I wanted something I got it, right there and then. And if other people got in the way then they simply had to go. But deep down I knew things had to change, but I thought, 'What's the hurry, there's always tomorrow.' Well, HIV took care of that thinking. Looking back it would have been nice to have had a choice, but even so I have no regrets. Don't get me wrong. I'm not sick in the head. It's just that now I have decided to really live again, to take care of myself and those relationships that I have taken for granted. You don't *have* to die of AIDS.' [32]

Positive or negative, there is no copyright on tragedy or on courage. Yes, the old days have passed, the carnival of '69 may well have receded into the background but we gay men still have a lot of singing to do. In the face of so many losses, with greater urgency than ever, we need to transcend our differences, raise high our rainbow flags and join in our own international anthem:

> I am what I am and what I am needs no excuses.
> I deal my own deck sometimes the ace, sometimes the deuces.
> It's one life and there's no return and no deposit;
> one life so it's time to open up your closet.
> Life's not worth a damn 'til you can say,
> 'Hey, world, I am what I am.' [33]

Part Two

Only connect
the passion and the prose
and both will be exalted
and human love will be seen at its height.
Live in fragments no longer.

– E. M. Forster, *Howards End*

HOLY, HOLY, HOLY

Holy God,
Holy and Vulnerable,
Holy and Dying One,
Have mercy upon us!

– An alternative *Trisagion*

IT could be argued that AIDS presents no new theological
questions, but rather all the old ones in a more acute form.
It is true that much ink has already been spilt concerning
the relationship between Creator and creature, God's
action in human history, evil, suffering, innocence and
guilt, the exercise of human freedom and responsibility,
and death. [34] Yet I would argue that AIDS presents the
world and therefore the Church with an unprecedented
social and theological crisis. The uniqueness of AIDS, especially for the Christian community, is that it strings together
by necessity, and dares to name in one sentence, all the
taboos which bid us hold our breath – God, sex and death.
References to the first and third of these are fairly ubiqui-
tous in the teaching and preaching life of the Christian
community. But sex and sexuality, which are difficult
enough to handle on their own, more awesome still when
sandwiched between God and death, are at the height of
the challenge that HIV/AIDS poses to faith. It is the blending
of these key ingredients that makes the AIDS experience

39

unique and theologically terrifying. Given such a cocktail, AIDS spirituality can never be simply a variation on a well-established theme.

Even though AIDS might throw God, sex and death together in an unwelcome trinity, when taken separately each individual dimension presents more than enough theological challenges. Such questions as the nature, gender and personality of God, the place of the body and the role and setting for genital intimacy, death, judgement, heaven and hell have all been well aired over the years, yet without definitive answers.

Taken as couplets, the Christian tradition has seemed to be more at ease (at least theologically speaking) in connecting God and death. The paradigm of the Incarnation which reaches its fulfilment in the surrender to death of the God-Man Jesus leaves the Church in the very clear position of interpreting dying in the light of God's own participation in human finitude which is ultimately crowned in Resurrection glory.

Attempts to handle God and sexuality have proven more troublesome both doctrinally and pastorally. Controversy over such issues dominated the first five Christian centuries, only to be resolved at the level of theology at the Council of Chalcedon (451 CE), which affirmed as orthodox faith the full corporeal reality of the sexually embodied Christ and denounced deviations from that truth as heresy. The ensuing centuries bear witness to the reception of this insight in doctrine, creed and worship. But there is little evidence to suggest that this ever been translated into day to day spirituality. Rather, it would seem that Christianity has never really decided whether it is *pro-* or *anti*-body. We have had theologies of the body, but little body theology.

Likewise, celibate theologians have treated us to weighty tomes on the theology of sexuality but sexual theology remains virgin territory. I am continually mystified by the fact that the sexual embodiment which was good enough for Jesus Christ and intrinsic to his holiness is often ignored, usually suppressed but all too seldom embraced in the wholeness/holiness of those who bear His name. Surely it is about time that Christian living (spirituality) caught up with Christian speaking (Christology) and denounced docetism. [35]

But God, sex, and death, all three together is an unwelcome trinity indeed, a mind-blowing cocktail. What would happen if we dared to keep them together? Presuming that we leave aside the hackneyed line, 'God punishes certain forms of sexual behaviour with death,' what might we say? What verbs dare we place between these nouns? How would we string these three components together without falling into either fundamentalism or theological mathematics? Need there be a connection, less still an implicit causation theory lurking in the wings?

The most striking exposition of this trinity that I have come across is not verbal but visual. Located opposite one of London's busiest HIV testing and treatment clinics for gay men, Brompton Cemetery offers a sobering challenge to those who would use its central avenue as a shortcut from the gay village of Earls Court to the HIV clinic in Fulham. Here, where thousands lie buried beneath stone crosses, in the shadow of people dying with AIDS related illness, gay men cruise and have sex among the graves. This is Holy Trinity, Brompton, where God, sex and death are all present. Psychologists could have a field day!

What is going on here? Why do some of our gay

brothers cruise the living among the dead? Almost definitely some of them are living with the virus, perhaps picking it up on the way to or from a check up. What does this mean at a time when we could not be more aware that some sexual practices are life-threatening and potentially death-dealing? And is it not ironic that in the anonymous sexual encounters that take place in that cemetery, semen, the life force, should be spilt and enter into the death space? What has this to say about gay men's spirituality?

Is it that being gay and being sexual has brought us into such a familiarity with death that we no longer shun the grave? Echoing St Paul, has death lost its power over us? Or do we seek to become acquainted with the inevitable? Or again is the choice of venue, this sexual playground, itself an act of defiance, a silent yet nonetheless eloquent protest, a refusal to give in and be beaten? Is it an expression of a deeply felt need to maintain some continuity with carefree living as it was before the advent of AIDS? How far is denial at work, a refusal to acknowledge and act upon what we now know?

Hard though the challenge may be, for the positively gay Christian intent on pursuing anything other than a schizo-phrenic spirituality, the trinitarian charge – God, sex and death – demands a hearing and a jury within his very body. Nowhere has spirituality seen such a challenging incarna-tion as here in the broken bodies of those who follow an embodied God and whose own bodies house a sexually transmitted virus over which they have no control. This chaos is indeed significant. Questions abound: answers are rare. Yet many go believing. Perhaps, were we able to understand, we would not need faith. Perhaps we are too weak not to believe. To live without the comfort of answers, either definitive or provisional, is to find a place within the tradition of contemplative waiting, a very old tradition become more acute in modern circumstances. Embracing a way that refuses to let go of the questions, that doggedly believes without seeing, are two authentic signs of the 'Spirit-ed' origins of AIDS spirituality.

God, sex, and death. Who knows when the cocktail will explode? When it does, vulnerable God, have mercy upon us.

Song Eight

WHERE IS YOUR GOD?

My tears have become my food,
by night and by day,
while all around me ask continually,
'Where now is your God?'

— from Psalm 42

THOMAS Merton, writer and contemplative monk, included in one of his books a photograph of an industrial crane from which a hook is suspended. The daring caption reads, 'The only known photograph of God.' Just as I will never know the motive behind the writing on the convent wall, so Merton's curious juxtaposition of image and text teases the mind. Whatever his intent, his foray into theological engineering seems particularly apt at a time when AIDS causes many of us to feel how precarious is our own condition, dangling in mid-air between — hopefully — heaven above and — certainly — earth beneath. It prompts us to ask, 'Can the structure bear the strain? Will we be dropped? How much longer can we hold on?'

Then I ask myself if I am taking Merton too seriously and failing to recognise that what we thought was a hook is in fact an inverted question mark. Maybe the great monk and mystic was playing the jester in more ways than one.

Back in my university days, when I believed that theology had the answers to life's mysteries, I attended a striking series of seminars on Holocaust Theology given by a sabbatical scholar from the United States. Speaking with the passion of personal experience, he sobered our theological enthusiasm with the thought that, in the light of the Jewish Holocaust, the only theological discourse that could escape the charge of blasphemy was that which could be uttered in the presence of burning babies. A grotesque yet gripping image. If I understood him correctly, he was bringing to our attention two fundamental theological principles: first, nothing is outside the realm of God, and second, the necessity for any talk of God to take full cognizance of the most brutal realities of life. He went on to say that if in the face of such atrocities theology could find nothing to say, then it must remain silent. [36]

To claim a connection between what happened to the Jews in Nazi Germany and what is happening to gay men in our time may be controversial,but it is not without substance. [37] Let it never be forgotten that the men with the yellow stars were in the same concentration camps as the men with the pink triangles. Remember first the Jews. As a people they shared a religious and collective identity, set apart from others, promised God's special care and protection while, paradoxically, undergoing repeated persecution and scapegoating on account of that special status. The experience of 'ethnic cleansing' to the extent of six million men, women, and children bespeaks a crisis of unimaginable proportions. What was burned in the camps was their hope, their future, and their identity. What was it about being Jewish that their very existence should arouse such indiscriminate hatred and murderous intent? Had they not been persecuted enough? How much longer would they be cast in the role of scapegoat? Where was God as they watched their children starve, heard their women scream, and saw their men sink in to despair? Was this the price of being chosen? Had God broken his covenant?

If you have lived through the AIDS years with any sensitivity, it is not hard to see the parallels. The surviving Jews of post-war Europe are still not free of threat, nor are gay men in the shadow of AIDS. Having emerged from the long exile of personal and collective estrangement, our very existence is at risk. As gay men we have carried our share of the consequences of the world's evils, and the reward is a terrible disease and the scapegoating that has accompanied it. What price survival? Is it really a blessing to be alive when tormented with a scale of loss unimaginable to most of our contemporaries? To have undergone more grief and survived more deaths in these last few years than any one individual could be expected to endure in a lifetime leaves us ambivalent about the *blessing* of being spared.

Life as we have known it under the dark cloud of HIV has transformed us beyond recognition. As Andrew put it to me, 'I used to insist on buying CDs that had a ten-year guarantee, but I gave up (and pocketed the difference) when it dawned on me that ten years is at least double my own expected shelf-life.' Looking through photographs of a party barely two years ago, Peter counts three out of twenty-five friends alive today. Nick is desperate to have a new relationship, but dare he risk losing again, having buried two lovers in five years? For the first time in his life Sean is earning enough to make the transition from an extortionate rent to a moderate mortgage, but he dares not live beyond today since '*anything* could happen'.

Will Odets, a psychotherapist working with gay men in San Francisco, adds his voice to the innumerable Andrews, Peters, Nicks, and Seans we each know. Reflecting after a dinner party given by friends who seem unaffected by 'life in the shadow', he muses:

> We [gay men] have come to live with a different set of expectations and assumptions about life, about what it means and what the possibilities are. We have a different sense of time, and of possible futures and the lack of them, and a different sense of what is important and what is not ... It is as if we move through our troubled world walking in deep sand, while our hosts walk on paved roads – perhaps not gold, but firm, relatively clean, and trustworthy nevertheless. What was so apparent (in our hosts) during that dinner was their ease, their easy sense of expectation, and their trust that each step would follow the last, and that the road actually went somewhere. We have so little of that left. We move with so much more effort, and do it with so much doubt about its purpose. Too many men have already vanished, and too many more will surely follow. We live in a world of survivors – we hope – but also a world of ghosts,who, like invisible housemates, invade our solitude and complicate our lives. In our trek across the sand, we must negotiate paths between and around them, and between and around our feelings about them. This is the shadow that all gay men now live – and, if possible, love – in, whether they can acknowledge it or not, and it will remain a part of who we are for as long as we are each alive. [38]

What kind of God-talk will speak to Andrew, Peter, Nick, and Sean? Can it say anything to us who walk on quicksand, who stumble through the thick fog of ghosts which enshroud us? What has theology to say when the thud of bodies falling to the ground is muffled by the tinkling of ice in cocktails? [39] The psalmist is right, in this time of AIDS: 'My tears have become my food by night and by day, while all around me ask continually, "Where now is your God?"'

WHAT'S IT ALL ABOUT?

Should I scream and shout,
should I speak of love,
let my feelings out?
I never thought I'd come to this.
What's it all about?

— Mary Magdalene's song
from *Jesus Christ Superstar* [40]

AT the beginning of December 1995, following a sudden
deterioration of health, my dear friend Paul was admitted
to the AIDS ward of a central London hospital. His wife
Sarah telephoned to tell me that they had received bad
news and would appreciate a visit. Some time prior to this
Paul had explained to me how he had escaped one death
sentence under Idi Amin in Uganda, only to be given
another one – HIV – in the promised land of England. Over
the two years that we had known each other we had
become friends, and I had been received into the family
home as an honorary uncle to his five young children.

Arriving at the hospital, I discovered that Paul had been
diagnosed with PML, a rare form of aids related illness, for
which prognosis is not good and treatment barely effective.
Although no one would answer the inevitable question,
'How long has he got?' it was obvious from the nurses'
manner that there was cause for concern. We three sat
there: Paul, in a grief-filled silence too deep for words,

Sarah, soon to be a widow, wondering aloud how she was going to tell her five young children that their Dad would be dead by Christmas, and me, the professional AIDS pastor, silent, bewildered, aching within and without.

As the afternoon wore on, I went to the hospital chapel to draw breath and to be silent. I found to my amazement that the enormous painting of the victorious Risen Christ by Veronese, which dominates the back wall, was missing. How disturbingly appropriate that seemed. I had just come from one of the most painful and meaningless of human situations, seeking respite and solace in the house of God, and it was empty. There was nothing and no one there. There *was* no Resurrection, only a blank wall with holes indicating where the image of the death-defying Risen Christ had once hung. As I sat there, pondering Paul, Sarah, and the children, my eyes glued to this *nothingness*, I wondered if this was indeed the most true and profound theological statement I had ever encountered in my whole theological career. The Real Absence!

As T. S. Eliot noted, 'human kind cannot bear very much reality,' [41] and so, true to form, I quickly retreated into distraction and speculation. If it was appropriate that the Resurrection was missing from a hospital which knows so much about the wastage of human life through AIDS, what would I put in its place? What depiction of Christ would neither underestimate his identity nor belittle the seriousness of the human dilemma? In a setting so very familiar with emaciated youths and sobbing partners, what image of Christ would suffice? [42]

Various images ran through my mind. 'Christ the light of the world'? All I could see was 'the encircling gloom'. 'Christ the King'? Where is the kingly glory in the -

degradation of night sweats and constant diarrhoea? 'Christ the friend of sinners'? No thank you, that card has been overplayed in the AIDS scenario. 'Christ crying over the loss of his friend Lazarus'? 'Christ betrayed, abandoned, mocked, insulted, left to bleed to death on a cross'? Maybe, but what consolation does it bring to know that 'as it was in the beginning, is now, and ever shall be '?

If I *had* to choose an image of Christ, it would be drawn from the traditional picture of Jesus in the garden of Gethsemane. The experience of Jesus then, and that of many who live with AIDS now, converge in the loneliness of facing one's destiny, the apparent *sleep* of those you thought you could count on when you needed them most, the bargaining and beseeching – take it away, take it away, the delivery unto death through physical intimacy – a kiss, lovemaking, and at least the possibility of inner surrender and yielding to your fate in such a way that you walk into the arms of death, no longer with resistance or anger, but with the serenity of a free heart.

In pictorial form, the image firmly lodged in my mind is that depicted in the thirteenth-century carved crucifix that hangs in the chapel of the Javier Castle in northern Spain. The artist's sculpting genius is excelled only by his theological insight as he portrays Christ dying with a smile of utter serenity on his face. This is no soppy downplaying of the reality of ignominious suffering, rather is it the anticipation this side of the grave of Resurrection promise. Through his surrender, Christ the Victim is already Christ the Victor.

For some people living with HIV/AIDS the journey from victim to victor, oppressed to free, survivor to thriver, is the experience of a powerful life-enhancing conversion and spiritual transformation. While such people may no longer be looking to the churches to interpret, still less validate, their experience, the Christian community can ill afford to ignore such truly grounded and embodied spirituality.

Having said all that, if I had my way I would still leave that wall blank!

MELT US, MOULD US

Spirit of the living God,
fall afresh on us.
Spirit of the living God,
fall afresh on us.
Melt us, mould us,
fill us, use us.
Spirit of the living God,
fall afresh on us.

— Michael Iverson

AFTER years of putting work before family – a classic pastoral trait – I decided to make amends at least as far as my nieces and nephews were concerned, and have a go at being a *good* uncle. When my new resolution was put to the test by an invitation to Gary's Confirmation, I girded my loins and set off for Edinburgh.

As a cradle Catholic I am accustomed to being told what to do and what to think, but this was the first time I had been told where to sit! First to arrive, I duly took my place in the pew assigned to our family and dutifully moved along one bottom's worth each time another member of the clan arrived. So diligent were my efforts to accommodate that by the time the Mass began I had conceded my 'front stalls' view of the high altar for a huge pillar six inches in front of me. Cut off from the sanctuary, from all that was happening, and from all around me, unable to see anything other than this lump of 'church', my mind inevitably wandered back to my own confirmation more than twenty-five years earlier.

The ceremony brought me not only nostalgia but also pain, as I reflected on all those years since 'receiving the Spirit'. Little did I know when I knelt before the bishop in 1969 that the community which seemed so eager to confirm me in my faith would so soon deny the presence of that Spirit in my life and discipleship when as an adult I embraced my homosexuality. Suddenly the Roman version of 'good news to the poor' rang out with statements that only just stopped short of telling me that it was not only my love-making but also my very being that was morally evil and intrinsically disordered. My kind should not be allowed to meet on church premises, even for meetings of a pastoral nature, and I belonged in a catalogue with the mentally ill. What hurt most was that this was said *in the name of love* by the community of liberation. [43]

What made the occasion of my nephew's Confirmation in 1995 so acutely painful was the fact that the presiding bishop, Keith Patrick O'Brien, Archbishop of St Andrews and Edinburgh, had been forced under pressure from the Vatican to withdraw his ecclesiastical approval from one of the very few helpful educational responses to HIV to have emerged from the Roman Catholic Church in the United Kingdom. [44] The Church's dirty laundry had made the headlines in both the national and the religious press, all of which I had followed with a heavy heart. But nothing could have prepared me for the impact of being confronted with the authority of the Church in the person of the arch-bishop, at one and the same time *confirming* the faith (of my nephew) and *negating* my belief and loyalty, along with that of my gay brothers living with AIDS.

Sadly, the educational controversy, together with the homophobia that issues from the ecclesiastical powerhouses of Rome and Canterbury, are only secondarily concerned with sexual morality. Hidden behind a veneer of *decency* is the substantial issue of the use and abuse of authority. As far as the Roman Catholic Church is concerned, the present Bishop of Rome has used the command to Peter, 'Strengthen the brethren,' to make it well nigh impossible for so many Catholics to remain in the Church. Gay men are only one in a long list of marginalised groups. [45]

I say this as one who still loves the Church but who is increasingly ashamed of what she is doing in the name of love. Many of my gay friends have seen Peter's boat heading for the rocks and have jumped ship. So far I have refused to join them, believing as I do in the efficacy of my own Baptism and Confirmation: this means that I too possess the gift of the Spirit, I too am an ikon of Christ, and I too have a gospel of liberation to proclaim. I am greatly saddened that so many of my gay friends and those I have worked with have felt rejected by the Church. In four years of burying people who have died from AIDS related illnesses, I met plenty of baptised and confirmed Christians, but only once have I been asked to arrange a religious funeral. What is the Spirit saying to the churches in that?

In those two hours up against a true pillar of the Church, cut off from the holy place by more than stone, something broke in me, the fruit of which includes this book. Those six constricted inches brought me to ponder the possibility that in 'outing' closeted and oppressive gay priests and bishops who continued to preach their hostile message, Peter Tatchell and his colleagues at *Outrage* might well be 'intrinsically morally ordered' towards the good. After all we are supposed to believe that 'the truth will set you free.' Perhaps the time has come for gay and lesbian Christians loudly and clearly to denounce those they have protected as their pastors for colluding with the oppression of the poor (the pressing down of those who then have no power to act or take responsibility for their actions). Maybe 'outing' the priests and bishops is the only way forward. On the day of judgment the question will not be, 'Did you do what Rome or Canterbury told you?' but 'How did you treat your hungry, lonely, sick, imprisoned neighbour?' And there will be no mitre or pallium, nor any other form of fig leaf, behind which either the hierarchy of the Church or the gay community will be able to hide their nakedness or their shame at failing to heal the wounds of the world.

FORGIVE OUR FOOLISH WAYS

Dear Lord and Father of mankind,
Forgive our foolish ways!
Reclothe us in our rightful mind,
In purer lives thy service find,
In deeper reverence praise.

– John Greenleaf Whittier (1807–92)

WHEREAS the Church has a wonderful record of pastoral care and support for those affected by sickness or loss, gay people have often found that in the context of aids this ministry tends to be qualified, conditioned, or restricted because of moral disapproval of actions by which the virus is transmitted. Experience suggests that objections to sexual behaviour become, in practice, objections to the people concerned. As a gay Catholic I will need a lot of convincing that a description of my love-making in the language of 'intrinsic moral evil' does not also colour an estimation of me as a person. Our attitude to drug-dealing is similar: the fact of the activity influences our estimation of drug-dealers and our relationships with them.

Ironically, despite the dualism encapsulated in the tag, 'Love the sinner, hate the sin', some parts of the Christian Church have responded with alacrity, dedication, and vigour to the challenge of AIDS. In setting up hospices and specialised ministries to people living with AIDS, Christians have given shape to their gospel vocation to heal

and care for the sick. Many clergy and members of religious communities have taken this up as their full-time
ministry, resourced through the generosity of religious insti-
tutes, local congregations, and trust funds. [46] But while
this is exemplary it is not without irony.

Why is it that the Church can be so committed to caring
for me as a gay man when I am sick and needy but cannot
find a good word for me when I am well, loving, and
empowered? Is the Church interested in the real me, or
only in my sick body? A ministry directed to my whole
body, let alone to my total being, would have to recognise
how all-pervasive is the sexual-spiritual nature of that
being. Perhaps the real healing in this time of AIDS will not
be of the as yet incurable infection of the human immuno-
deficiency virus but of the dualistic theology of a Church
which would isolate sexual acts from their human agents.

The Church's commitment to healing is indeed partial,
in a similar way to the pro-life stance that stops at birth and
fails to include nuclear disarmament. But it is a start. It is
for you and me to insist on more, and to encourage the
Church to go beyond care for our bodily wounds to heal
those of our soul, so damaged by the homophobic atmos-
phere in which we live. A commitment to that dimension of
healing would see the Church clearly and unreservedly
'coming out' on the side of those who oppose the stigmati-
sation and exclusion of gay people. Until she does so, it
makes little sense to nurse people back to physical health
only to return them to 'negative, hostile, and germ-ridden
social and psychological environments' where they have
little chance of flourishing. [47]

I doubt whether the Church is ready for such a
significant *volte face*, since a thoroughgoing commitment to

healing would necessarily involve an acknowledgment and repentance of its own complicity in the oppression of gay people. The Church may issue pronouncements that decry the physical violence of 'queer bashing', but colludes with the emotional violence implicit in descriptions of 'intrinsic moral disorder'. Negative diatribes hardly contribute to the process of healing.

It comes as no surprise that many HIV-positive people have responded to the Church's 'falling short of the ideal' by creating new communities which live out the kingdom values so often lacking in that Church: care for the weakest, defence of the vulnerable, opposition to injustice, inclusion of all, the promotion of human dignity. Among our own number, infected and affected by the virus, we have sought out and, where absent, established networks of compassion, care, mutual support, and hope. Through the sharing of weakness new strength has been found. From the mutual sense of despair new hope has emerged. In this new covenant community of those who have lost so much already, where CVs and status symbols are cast aside, together with all those other masks which veil us from each other, only the raw wounded nakedness of humanity-encouraging-humanity is tolerable. Where 'deep calls to deep' there is neither widow, nor stranger, nor orphan. Is this not witness enough to the possibility of rising from the dead?

As Peter Baelz has commented:

> It is not surprising, then, if the structures of the Church are rejected in favour of a community of the spirit, preservation in favour of vulnerability, order in favour of disorder. Nor is there any need to deny that the Spirit of God is indeed present amidst the chaos and confusion, breaking forth in new

and unlikely places, anywhere and everywhere carrying out his anonymous and life-giving work. God's kingdom is broader and deeper than the visible Church. The spirit of life and love is not limited to its structures, or even to its sacraments.' [48]

Part Three

Only connect
the passion and the prose
and both will be exalted
and human love will be seen at its
height.
Live in fragments no longer.

– E. M. Forster, *Howards End*

Song Twelve

YOU'LL NEVER WALK ALONE

When you walk through a storm
keep your chin up high
and don't be afraid of the dark.
At the end of the storm
is a golden sky
and the sweet silver song of a lark.
Walk on through the wind,
walk on through the rain,
though your dreams be tossed and blown.
Walk on, walk on, with hope in your heart,
and you'll never walk alone,
you'll never walk alone.

– Oscar Hammerstein [49]

IN 1987, a man named Richard came to live in the rectory of the Anglican parish of St Clement's, Notting Dale, where David Randall was the parish priest. Richard had come to London from the United States where he had contracted the mysterious virus, then known as HTL III, later and ever since as HIV. At that time, gay men in London who were affected by HIV were beginning to meet together and pool whatever resources they had to support one another, to campaign for good quality care for people suffering from this new disease, and to stand up against the fear, prejudice, and ignorance of society. Many of the self-help groups associated with this pandemic were in their first fervour staffed by worried gay men who rallied to do their bit for their bit for the cause. Like many 'positive' men, Richard went from group to group, from clinic to clinic, from one advice centre to another. He received excellent advice on the financial implications of his illness, on his housing problems, on free travel passes around London, and on the legal aspects of immigration. In fact he could find help for almost everything he needed as an HIV positive man.

One problem remained. Richard was a committed Christian who believed that 'man does not live by bread alone.' He had a *spirit* and he needed to talk with other *spirited* people about what HIV and AIDS meant for his faith, his relationship with God, and his spirituality. He tried speaking to people from the churches. But, with remarkably few exceptions, they did not want to know. After all, he was gay. He tried talking about his faith and spiritual life to the HIV positive gay men that he met in the various AIDS centres, but there seemed to be a taboo there about God. Many of them had good reason to be angry with the Church, having felt condemned and rejected. But Richard did not give up. Little by little he discovered that he was not alone. A hint here, an off-the-cuff remark there, brought him to others who shared his spiritual questioning but were afraid of talking openly about it for fear of seeming to collude with those who were oppressing their brothers. It seemed there was only one thing more lonely than being gay in the Christian community, and that was being Christian in the gay community.

And that was how CARA came to be born. Responding to Richard and to many like him, David Randall dreamed of creating a safe place where those affected by HIV could explore their spirituality in the light of this new moment, and together draw strength to face the future. But David's dream included an outward thrust as well. CARA, by its very existence, and by its commitment to education, would be a community and a place where the churches could wrestle with the challenges that people like Richard present.

It was not that the churches had been silent on HIV/AIDS: far from it. People had spoken loudly and confidently, declaring that AIDS was God's punishment on homosexuals who refused to obey God's will. How anyone would want to live with a God who acts in this way, never mind love or praise him, I have no idea. But here was an easy answer to a complex question. What made it worse was its appeal to all the monotheistic faiths as well as to all the Christian denominations. Churches with centuries of disagreement on almost everything else suddenly found themselves agreeing that AIDS was God's just condemnation. And Jews and Muslims agreed.

Those who disagreed did not shout, and their stance was rarely reported. The fundamentalists had money, influence, and power: so their message got through.

Those who maintained that the issue was complex and who held on to belief in a God of loving mercy were ignored.

CARA maintains the twin strands of David's pastoral and educational ministry to this day. Its belief is that the continuing daily encounters, a privilege for those engaged in such pastoring, ground its educational activity and give it authority. CARA is simply a storytelling community made up of those who live in the 'thin place' between life and death. There is no room for pretence or for hiding behind fig leaves. As David would say, 'The issues that HIV/AIDS presents are fundamentally our *own* issues, not someone else's.'

CARA's current director, Mike Way, put it poignantly: We are those who have

> heard the silent beating of the wings of love on the cloud of unknowing. [That cloud] is our life affected so deeply and profoundly by a virus. It is within this cloud that we shall find our buried treasure, our wisdom, our meaning, and our destiny. But we need to have the 'wings of love' – first, love of our self – to know who we are, to treasure our self, and to have the courage to celebrate the gift of our self, to our self. This is but the beginning. But it is a vital and demanding beginning, which enables us to be healers rather than abusers, and it takes time, honesty, and courage. It is only this kind of love which can then begin to flow out in reconciliation and hope to our world. [50]

In fifteen years of pastoral ministry in parishes, schools, and spirituality workshops in the UK, Spain, and South America, I have never encountered so much spirituality amidst so little religion, so much kingdom-living amidst such infrequent church-going as in these four years at CARA. I would agree with a brother Jesuit that many HIV positive people use the words 'spiritual' and 'spirituality' with greater familiarity and ease than many of my colleagues in church defined ministries. The resources, methods, and practices may well be eclectic, but none can deny that the experience of having to contend with issues of such fundamental importance as sexuality and mortality has led many to acknowledge a deeper dimension of their being, for they have 'had the experience without missing the meaning', 'reoriented the direction of their lives, anticipated their future with hope, and become reconciled with the past, and are thus able to reach out to others in service and love.' [51]

LOVE UNKNOWN

My song is love unknown,
My Saviour's love to me,
Love to the loveless shown
That they might lovely be.

– Samuel Crossman (*c.* 1624–84)

A NEW way of 'being church' demands a new way of relating to one another. Most traditional models of ministry, for example, imply a relationship of intrinsic difference between the parties involved. Along comes the pastor equipped with his training, recognised social status, and privileged access to the holy places (Sanctuary) and holy things (Scriptures, Sacraments), calls on one of 'his' flock in need, and dispenses wisdom, pastoral counsel, or sacramental grace to comfort and raise her up. Such a framework, however seemingly hallowed by history, is potentially abusive, for it provides pastors who have voracious appetites for 'helping the needy' to do so while remaining out of touch with their own wounded inner selves. The opposite danger to pastoral overkill is pastoral neglect, especially where the pastor's words and ministrations are not greeted with the acclaim to which privilege has accustomed him.

Like sex, ministry is a high risk activity and should be handled with care. AIDS ministry is certainly no exception. Those of us who dare to be involved in it must be brutally honest with ourselves as to why it is that we are drawn to be around people who are suffering and dying, often in the most gruelling of circumstances. We need to listen not only to ourselves, but also to trusted friends and supervisors, lest we become pastoral or sexual voyeurs. If we are honest we have to admit that there is nothing as juicy as a bit of AIDS work on the side to jazz up a boring parochial ministry or to provide the fizz in a bland sabbatical. What religious order is there that does not exploit the fact that one of its sisters works with people with AIDS? For good or bad, involvement with AIDS has come to be a contemporary expression of what religious communities, following liberation theology, call 'the preferential option for the poor', and an indication of the street credibility and trendiness of an individual pastor or community.

With one foot in direct pastoral care and the other in training others for AIDS ministry, I have from time to time asked people living with HIV/AIDS what they would like to say to pastors. Here are some of their replies:

— Speak to us in our own language, not in your own. We are persons with AIDS, not clients, service users, or victims.
— We are *living with* AIDS, not *dying of* AIDS.
— I am not 'your little boy'.
— Don't judge us, but accept us. Don't ask too many questions. We'll tell you what we want you to know.
— Don't classify us into two groups — the 'poor innocents' and those who brought HIV on themselves.
— Don't come thinking you have all the answers. We might have something to teach you.
— Don't say that you know what it is like, or how we feel.

You haven't got a clue.
- Don't make unrealistic promises. We've been let down enough.
- Don't intensity our pain by your own inability to cope with unresolved issues: sexuality, loneliness, powerlessness …
- Don't be frightened of us. We won't infect you.
- Don't presume familiarity. We have boundaries too.
- Don't love me for *Christ's* sake. Love me for *my* sake.
- Allow us to talk of AIDS as a spiritual journey.
- Don't come as an amateur social worker or counsellor. We have enough of them wanting to intervene. Come as a pastor, as a person of faith.
- We are looking for God too, but not necessarily in the places where the Church has hidden him.
- Don't claim copyright on God or on spirituality. Listen to our experience. Don't push.
- Make sure you don't need us more than we need you.
- Why are you doing this work? What is in it for you?

Those last two questions still haunt me. They were put to me in my very first week at CARA by Johnathon, whom I can describe only as a man with far seeing eyes. There I was, forty shades of green in the presence of someone who refused to play the poor victim to me the eager helper. The goal posts had moved. I wanted to help. I needed to help. Every fibre of my being had been programmed, de-programmed, and re-programmed to help. But the rug was suddenly and completely snatched from under my pastoral feet. In his own inimitable way, Johnathon brought home to me the truth of those words of David's, 'The issues that HIV and AIDS presents are fundamentally our own issues.' Face to face with my own sexuality, spirituality, addictive cycles, and inability to beat death, the question shifted from 'How can I *help* Johnathon?' to 'Who am *I*, what do *I* live for, what does all this mean to me?'

I was flung headlong into the powerlessness of God.

> The heart of the Christian message is that the most salvific moment in the history of the world was when one man was pinned to a cross unable to do anything for anybody about anything. Until we can come to the point of living in the presence of unbearable inability to do anything, I don't think we've really entered into the presence of a crucified God. [52]

This model of ministry, this way of being one with another which is based not on the acquisition of skills and endless cycles of training, but on the shared plight of powerlessness, is neatly summarised in a saying of the Aboriginal Peoples:

> If you have come to help me, you are wasting your time. But if you have come, because your liberation is bound up with mine, then, come, let us walk together.

What AIDS has taught me is that we are all in this together. There is no divide between helper and helped. The issue is not even HIV or AIDS but *life* and how we live it. As someone with AIDS put it, 'Dying is the easy part. I can manage that myself. It's my living I need some help with.'

AIDS is a great leveller. I would say that it has made me more human. It has certainly taught me that the most important issues in life are much deeper than those of which church we belong to, and that ministry is a matter of the heart regardless of commissioning or ordination. When we begin to live in the *today* of life with all its shadows and mess, in which uncertainty prevails, there is little room for the clutter of qualifications with which we defend ourselves and dare to call ourselves pastors. Give me a pilgrim any day!

Song Fourteen

A GOSPEL TO PROCLAIM

We have a gospel to proclaim,
Good news for men in all the earth!

– E. J. Burns (b. 1938)

IF there is any currency in the concept of the 'poor' being not merely recipients but agents of evangelisation, we can legitimately ask what 'good news' does the experience of gay men living with AIDS offer the Christian Church? We have already seen how AIDS is forcing us to look again at our traditional models of ministry. But what light does the struggle to grapple with questions of God, sex, and death, throw on our images of holiness?

AIDS spirituality counters the tendency of the Christian community to undermine the full corporeal, embodied, sexual nature of God's embrace of humanity in Jesus of Nazareth. While the doctrine itself has been condemned often enough, this pervasive heresy lives on psychologically through our imagining that Christ could never have assumed those elements of our humanity that we cannot accept in ourselves. Thus James Nelson:

> That Jesus should be a laughing, crying, sweating, urinating, defecating, orgasmic, sensuous bundle of flesh, just as we are, seems incomprehensible. The reverse is also true. Because we find it difficult to believe that God genuinely embraced total flesh in Jesus, we have trouble believing that incarnation can and does occur in us too. Lacking the conviction that God not

only blesses human flesh from afar but also intimately embraces and permeates the body-selves which we are, expressing divine presence and activity in the world through us, we find it difficult to incorporate our sexuality into our spirituality.

And he continues,

If we do not know the gospel in our bodies, we do not know the gospel. We either experience God's presence in our bodies, or not at all.' [53]

People living with AIDS challenge the Christian community to affirm and experience God's saving, creative, redeeming, and sanctifying presence in the flesh, in the intimacies of our sexual love-making, illness, and pain. AIDS spirituality challenges us in a particular way to accept the fleshly, here-and-now paschal aspects of Christian spirituality, the dying-and-rising Christ embodied in us. If the incarnation is about God committing himself without reserve to humanity, in total solidarity with all human beings, then people with AIDS can indeed be one of the many ikons waiting to be recognised in the contemporary world. Theirs is the face of Christ in the world today. There God hides and reveals himself.

Incarnation requires em-body-ment. So does transfiguration. One of the central paradoxes of the incarnation is that it occurs in unexpected places. So we meet and touch, hold and hug, laugh and cry. In this meeting of warm flesh we hear once more of a body broken, of blood poured out. Our hearts burn within us as we recognise him once again. And we are dumbfounded to find that our grief is tinged with joy.

*

Another aspect of AIDS spirituality is its stress on community. For many people, the experience of what it is to be gay, collectively undergone, together with the second bite of the apple (as ever ambiguous fruit) at the time of an HIV diagnosis, leads to a rediscovery of what lies at the heart of our individual and shared humanity. This is mediated through informal supportive networks of body-positive people, friends, partners, family, complementary therapists, and volunteers. Certainly the initial inspiration and impetus for such groups came from HIV positive gay men. What happens in these new 'communities' is that a safe place is created where nothing that is human is found to be strange, where the depths of fear and the desire for self-annihilation can be excavated in good company, and faith in the friendliness of the facts be affirmed 'this side of the Jordan'. As a founder member of CARA has written:

> What AIDS then appears to confirm, through the urgent drama of the apparently disastrous and wasteful deaths of many young people, is that the saving experience for an individual is mediated through a saving community. AIDS reminds Christians to be suspicious of any tendency to over-individualise or to privatise conversion, belief, or spiritual practice. Our faith is characteristically about membership and sharing. The kingdom is about a social or community view of our ultimate destiny. [54]

Is such a community any less saving and liberating than a monastic foundation or religious community? One has to think only of Alcoholics Anonymous and the plethora of self-help groups which base themselves on the 'twelve steps' to realise that groupings of people who are willing to engage in honest self-disclosure, and in the relationships that such a commitment to truth compels, 'come to believe that a Power greater than themselves can restore them (to wholeness).'[55]

Fuller living, the rediscovery – or perhaps the first discovery – of the God-given dignity of each and every human being, the courage to name and reject collusive relationships, the identification of structural oppression as well as of personal sin, the ability to name one's desires, the power to refute all tyrannies inflicted by the habitual patterns of self or others: all of this creates a mediating saving community out of the looming darkness and chaotic turmoil of the pandemic.

Implicit in this embodiment of community is a commitment to service and hospitality. Those repeatedly told that they did not belong are creating places of welcome and refuge open even to their old enemies. The love being shown by this community at a time when all its members could so easily bury their heads in self-absorption has to be reckoned with. There is a powerful energy at work.

And for those with eyes to see, something even more mysterious is happening. In the many gay men and lesbian women who have rallied to serve so generously 'stands in our midst one we do not know.' The S/stranger is delivering a message.

Bodily incarnate, community-serving, AIDS spirituality is also by nature paschal. The community of infected and affected keep alive the tradition of 'anamnesis' (active remembering) so central to the liturgical rhythms of Judaism and Christianity. In the telling of each one's story, accompanied by the reverent listening of all present, echoes of an old song about life in the face of death can be heard, reinterpreted, and reclaimed.

> There is no answer to the reality of death. But the subversive memory of life in death suggests that we can learn and live together up to a point, refusing to relinquish hold of one another, and so wresting some kind of new life from the living void from which we sprang and to which we all return.' [56]

But holiness is not only about harmony, reconciliation, and accepting everything as one's cross in life. So AIDS spirituality is also characterised by multi-levelled transformation. Continuing the work of Christ, it is immersed in the struggles of individuals and communities for freedom from all that crushes. At a personal level, this transformation is from tragedy to opportunity, from victimisation to fuller living. At the level of society, interwoven with the immediate alleviation of individual suffering, it finds expression in the political commitment to transform public attitudes and policies, to counter discrimination in health and social care, to protect the civil liberties of all persons with HIV/AIDS, and to defend all those living with disabilities. AIDS spirituality incarnates the service of faith and the promotion of justice. It is intrinsically morally ordered towards the kingdom.

Finally, the spirituality of HIV-positive people is *positive* spirituality. To put it another way, it is about empowerment. Bruno Holleran writes in one of CARA's annual reports:

> It is no coincidence that 'being positive' (with HIV) has come to mean 'living positively', enjoying, with tenderness and humour, the gift of each moment, sensing the life-giving power deeper than ourselves, rising from within ourselves. We find peace in a mystery of life deeper than we had imagined, the age-old mystery of new life arising out of death, both in

and around us today, and then (who knows?) beyond our present horizons. This is the testimony of courage and hope to be seen both in those infected by HIV and in those affected by it as carers and friends. It is also the dynamic perspective of ancient myth, and of all religious and monastic life. [57]

It is a paradox that the experience of darkness and death in ourselves, in God, and in our loved ones, can lead to an affirmation of life and hope. In a parallel and wonderful way, when we find a supportive community in which to open ourselves to our own vulnerability, weakness, and fear, however challenging and threatening it feels, we discover a new and extraordinary empowerment. More than anything else, the AIDS pandemic is an appeal for authenticity, a cry from apparent complete destruction bringing forth triumphantly the true greatness of the human spirit. What we have seen in the dark, we must speak in the light. What we have heard in whispers, we must proclaim from the housetops.

A SOLO SAXOPHONE

A song, played on a solo saxophone,
A crazy sound, a lonely sound,
A cry that tells us love goes on and on...

– from *Miss Saigon* [58]

A NEW community with its own style of ministry and emerging spirituality requires a new pattern of ritual and public expression. As the reality of AIDS impinges on our lives, bringing with it loss upon loss, bereavement after bereavement, any liturgy *must* be a place of truth, facing the pain and the mess and the unanswerable questions, with no sentimentality and no glib religious platitudes. In a pastoral encounter I may simply be alongside another human being, deflecting questions of meaning and significance back to the questioner. But in public liturgy we face the dilemma that whatever we say not only seeks to interpret the experience before us, but also places that interpretation in the shared space between us. If, as I have tried to suggest, anything that might be said in the context of AIDS is provisional, and that wisdom and truth are in the process of being made rather than given in advance, how can we be together in public ritual?

The problem is real, and there seem to be few places to which we can turn for help. Most forms of liturgy, Christian, Jewish, or any other, leave little room for the uncertain and the provisional. Among other things, liturgy has traditionally made a body of theological truths available to those who are not theologically literate in a complex and dramatic language of symbol, action, and word. How then can people who no longer know who their God is, who question God's existence, who struggle with God's seeming inability or unwillingness to make a difference, come together when there is no publicly shared truth, only myriad opinions, and no shared experience beyond the memory of the past, the bewilderment of the present, and the fear – possibly mixed with hope for the future? What will serve our needs?

My hunch is that we are being invited to live with silence. AIDS has provoked so many words, both of condemnation and of support. We have wound ourselves up so tightly, and we have been burned with the heat and frenzy of our activism. Maybe it is now time to sit still in our unknowing, with others in their unknowing. Maybe it is time to learn how important it is simply to wait. The liturgies which have proved most effective at CARA have not been those where the one presiding has tried to fit AIDS into some grand scheme and give it some meaning, but those when we have sat on the floor, as close as the carpet will allow to mother earth, from whom we come and to whom we will all return, and become still and silent together. All too well do we know that

'Words strain, crack, and sometimes break,
under the burden, under the tension,
slip, slide, perish, decay with imprecision,
will not stay in place, will not stay still.' [59]

So we use symbols: the red ribbon with its call to remember, resolve, and respond; the book of remembrance, with its names and photographs and personal messages; the flickering candles defeating the darkness in their own understated way; the CARA logo – the phoenix rising out of the ashes – which speaks of the new life which is emerging out of the darkness and destruction and which calls us to hope. Perhaps our most frequent ritual is the making of a circle. When we meet, whether for business or pleasure, we form a circle and invite each person to claim his or her space and be heard. It is a small, but not insignificant, outward expression of a deep inner understanding that the journey is shared, that there are no leaders with answers from outside, that our personal liberation is bound up with that of everybody else.

Funerals, or 'Celebrations of Life' as they are often called, are key ritual moments in our community life. We attempt to do publicly what in some ways we cannot do privately. People are encouraged to plan their own funerals, indicating the location, guest list, music, speakers, and who is to act as MC. A crucial question is whether or not a 'God word' is to be spoken, and if so, by whom. Most of the funerals I have conducted have not been conventionally religious, but rarely have people declined my offer of a spiritual word.

Given that the gay community contributes enormously to the world of art, music, and theatre, many of these celebrations of life have been more than a little 'over the top'. Yet that in itself seems entirely appropriate. You have only to think of those funerals taken by 'rent-a-vicar' who, despite never having met the deceased, waxes lyrical about her and in so doing convinces the rest of us that we must be in the wrong crematorium. He cannot possibly be speaking about the so-and-so in the coffin. The funeral is not the time to speak ill of the dead.

Of the many funerals I have conducted one stands out in particular. Patrick had been heavily involved in sado-masochism. His wardrobe, while extensive, contained only denim, leather, and chains. He lay in an open coffin, dressed accordingly. He was surrounded by all his friends, who were similarly attired. They were also variously chained to each other's bodies. Next to his coffin his partner had placed a circular wreath of white flowers, in the centre of which lay a barbie doll clad in a leather harness, her legs spread wide. One after another his friends spoke of his sexual prowess and of their memories both of taking drugs together and of their sexual exploits. It was one of the most honest rituals I had ever witnessed. It had no hint whatever of what might be called 'insurance policy funerals' where the deceased is suddenly transformed from the little devil he was into the angel he certainly was not, nor where the messiness of life is swept tidily away under the crematorium carpet, only to emerge once everyone has had enough to drink.

Patrick's funeral provided a ritual which allowed his partner and friends to do what they would have done if he himself had been there. It spoke of the continuity of the past and the present. It defiantly challenged convention and boldly stated Patrick's wish to go out as he came in, to be himself without compromise. Psychologically, what the funeral did for his friends and partner was to enable them to grieve, in the way most familiar to them, the very real person they had lost. The eulogies which spoke of his sexual flexibility were saying something profoundly important about their grief. There is something cathartic about saying what you've *really* lost in the death of a friend. How vital that is in the working through that loss.

At more conventional funerals we seem to mark the departure of the soul but not of the body. The *real* person has not been commemorated, and the coffin disappears mechanically and impersonally from our sight.

That Patrick's partner had approached what is an unashamedly Christian pastoral agency to conduct his funeral left me surprised and not a little proud. Towards the end of the 'service' I simply picked up some of the threads that had emerged and commented that if God was not in all of Patrick's life, then I had no idea where he was, nor did I want anything to do with Him. The leather clad congregation nodded. Their chains clanked, and Patrick went 'somewhere over the rainbow'.

Closing Bars

Only connect
the passion and the prose
and both will be exalted
and human love will be seen at its height.
Live in fragments no longer.

– E. M. Forster, *Howards End*

SINGING FOR OUR LIVES

We are a gentle, angry people,
and we are singing, singing for our lives...

We are weavers of new patterns,
and we are singing, singing for our lives...

– Holly Near [60]

WE positively gay and Christian men have plenty to celebrate and every need to sing. We have survived twenty centuries of contempt, hatred, and attempted annihilation by those who wield power in society, we have resisted the interpretation of our love as pathological, and we have refused to be silenced by those who feign copyright on the things of the Spirit. All this has been possible because others have been there before us. We belong to a great and noble tradition of men and women who would not settle for second best, who held on by their fingernails to a belief in the human and Christian dignity of every human being.

Many false prophets have arisen, preaching a fearful avenging God, but we have clung to that older and more biblically based picture of a man, fully sexual and fully alive, who was more at home with foot-washing than with passing judgment. The churches have sanitised that man in an attempt to make him 'holy', but we sense in him a familiarity with embodiment and death, intimacy and betrayal, love and violence. Even in his own lifetime religious leaders

85

tried to pin him down – on a cross – but he got up again. He is like that. So is spirituality. So are we. We have been through too much already for anyone to think that AIDS is going to beat us now.

We have seen more than our fair share of coffins, grave-yards, and tears. We know what tragedy, loss, stigma, and isolation mean. But every candlelit vigil, every collector's tin, every self-help group that defies cuts in funding, pro-claims our empowerment, strength, courage, and pride in living. We are indeed an angry people, angry at the lies that have been heaped upon us for as long as we can remember, angry with those who would banish us to live in darkened closets and the shadows of self-loathing, angry at those who would see us as less than human. Despite it all, we are also a *gentle* people, learning above all to be gentle with ourselves as we face up to how fragile we are, as we reclaim our past history, and as we live fully this present moment.

In the AIDS wards of our hospitals we live out our faith and love publicly. In our brothers who have been open and truthful about their sexuality, their HIV status, and their Christian allegiance, we present to the Church bodies that have been pricked with thorns, perhaps a truer Body of Christ than the one that so often does not live up to its name. We have certainly challenged the canonisation of dogma over the practice of love. As a tribe we have out-grown the infantile behaviour of 'keeping Mother (Church) good'. We have our own leaders now, and we are reclaim-ing the authority of the voice within. We bring our wounds to one another for healing, we forgive one another our sins, and we make Christ's eucharist together. Rejected by semi-naries and religious institutions, we make up more than our statistical proportion of the staff of the caring professions, and we minister grace and reconciliation to those who have lost their way and seek a new and more abundant life. Our song is wonderful, insistent, questioning, celebrating, searching, gentle, angry, and faith-filled. In this time of AIDS, with every fibre of our being we will go on singing, singing for our lives!

Coda

Because still on the youthful wing
   The scent of innocent beauty lies
   That touched by a stranger scatters and dies –

This love must I tenderly sing.

Yet since you think it a dirty thing,
   Have dragged it through mud and infamy,
   And kept it in the dark under lock and key -

This love will I freely sing.

To love's persecuted my song I bring,
   And to the outcast of our time,
   Since happy or not this love is mine -

This love dare I loudly sing.

         – John Henry Mackay, *The Nameless Love* [62]

NOTES

1   'The thief comes only to steal and kill and destroy, but I have come that
    you may have life and have it to the full.' John 10.10.

2   I am indebted to Tom McGuinness sj for this powerful image of God's
    reconciling action as witnessed in spiritual accompaniment and in the
    Sacrament of Reconciliation. The phrase appears in the song *Who But a
    God?* on the tape entitled *Exsultet*.

3   A view tragically still held by fundamentalists within Judaism, Islam, and
    Christianity. *The Times* of 15 August 1995 carried two articles side by side.
    The first called on all *true* Muslims to kill homosexuals. The second
    reported an Anglican vicar's refusal to baptise a child unless the proposed
    godfather, a committed gay Christian, was replaced. Similarly, when the
    Gay Games were held in Vancouver in 1990, a religious group took out a
    full-page newspaper advertisement calling the event 'The Sodomite
    Invasion', and prophesying an earthquake as a sign of divine disapproval.
    Either God did not keep his word, or the earth refused to oblige.

4   © The Provost and Scholars of King's College, Cambridge.

5   *Old Friends / Like It Was* from the musical *Merrily We Roll Along* by Stephen
    Sondheim. © 1981, 1983, 1984 by Revelation Music Publishing
    Corporation and Rilting Music Inc. Executive Offices, Suite 2110, 1270
    Avenue of the Americas, New York City, NY10020. International
    Copyright Secured. All Rights Reserved. Permission sought.

6   Cf. the writings of Matthew Fox, Jim Cotter, James Nelson. This section
    owes its inspiration to a stunning workshop given by Chris Roberts at a
    Spirituality Day for CARA in November 1994.

7   Henri J. Nouwen, *Lifesigns: Intimacy, Fecundity, Ecstasy in Christian Perspective*,
    Doubleday, New York, 1986, pp. 38-40. Permission sought.

8   *Memories / The Way We Were*, sung by the gay diva Barbra Streisand, by
    Alan Bergman and Marilyn Bergman, EMI Publishing, 127 Charing
    Cross Road, London WC2H 0EA. International Copyright Secured. All
    Rights Reserved. Permission sought.

9   John McNeill, *Taking a Chance on God*, Beacon Press, Boston, 1988,
    pp. 17-18.

10 Cf. Bernard Hoose, 'Sexual Ethics: Some Recent Developments', *The
    Way* 33 (1994), pp. 54-62.

11 This section owes much to Brian McNaught's eminently readable *On
    Being Gay: Thoughts on Family, Faith, and Love*, St Martin's Press, New York,
    1988, pp. 134-9.

12 Cf. Peter Brown, *The Body and Society: Men, Women, and Sexual Renunciation
    in Early Christianity*, Faber, London, 1990.

13   I am indebted for this section to John Laurisen's *Religious Roots of the Taboo on Homosexuality.*

14   © Paul Simon Music, 1619 Broadway, Suite 500, New York City, NY 10019. International Copyright Secured. All Rights Reserved.

15   Gordon Wakefield, *Spirituality* in ed. Gordon Wakefield, *A Dictionary of Christian Spirituality*, SCM Press, London, 1983, pp. 361, and S. H. Evans, *op. cit.*, pp. 13–16.

16   John Fortunato, *Aids: The Spiritual Dilemma*, HarperCollins Publishers Inc., San Francisco, 1987, pp. 7–8. © John E. Fortunato.

17   Segundo Galilea, 'The Spirituality of Liberation', *The Way*, 25 (1985), p. 190. Reproduced from *The Way* by permission of the Editors, Heythrop College, Kensington Square, London W8 5HQ.

18   Louis Dupré, *Transcendental Selfhood: The Loss and Rediscovery of the Inner Life*, Seabury Press, New York, 1976.

19   Paul Monette, *Becoming a Man: Half a Life Story*, Abacus, London, 1994, p. 1.

20   J. S. Spong, *Living in Sin? A Bishop rethinks sexuality*, HarperCollins Inc., San Francisco, 1988, p. 23. © Rt Revd John Shelby Spong.

21   Cf. Stephen Pattison, 'To the Churches with Love from the Lighthouse', in ed. James Woodward, *Embracing the Chaos: Theological Responses to AIDS*, SPCK, London, 1991, p.18, note 17.

22   Monette, *op. cit.*, p. 2.

23   From *Blood Brothers* by Willy Russel, © Willy Russel Music. Used with permisssion.

24   World Health Organisation, November 1996.

25   *The AIDS Letter* 59, 1997, p. 1.

26   Cf. Edward Norman, 'AIDS and the Will of God', Woodward, *op. cit.*, p. 89.

27   © Gene Raskin, Essex Music Group, 535 Kings Road, London SW10. Permission sought.

28   *The Perfect Love*, written by David for his lover Adam after receiving his AIDS diagnosis. Used with permission. All rights reserved.

29   © Wendy O'Mara. A mother responds to her daughter's HIV diagnosis. Saturday 14 October, 1995. Used with permission.

30   Søren Kierkegaard, *The Concept of Dread*, tr. Walter Lowrie, OUP, London, 1946. By permission of Oxford University Press.

31   As quoted in her recitation at Lewisham Town Hall 1988.